4:

MW00764218

Heather

Love,
Grandma

September 17, 2013

© 2012 by Barbour Publishing, Inc.

Written and compiled by Emily Biggers.

ISBN 978-1-61626-628-8

Published by Barbour Publishing, Inc., P.O. Box 719, Uhrichsville, Ohio 44683, www.barbourbooks.com

Our mission is to publish and distribute inspirational products offering exceptional value and biblical encouragement to the masses.

 Member of the
Evangelical Christian
Publishers Association

Printed in China.

It's a GRL Thing!

Txts 4 Her <3

BARBOUR
PUBLISHING

LOL = laugh out loud	A3 = anywhere, anytime, anyplace
24/7 = 24 hours a day, 7 days a week	ATB = all the best
BFF = best friend forever	HRT2HRT = heart to heart
URD1! = you are the one!	sweet<3 = sweetheart
(((H))) = big hug	FYI = for your information
JTLYK = just to let you know	1NAM = one in a million
BG = big grin	H&K = hugs and kisses
G/F = girlfriend	\&&&/ = princess
DF = dear friend	<\3 = broken heart
<333 = lots of love	ROTFL = rolling on the floor laughing
POAHF = put on a happy face	TTL = totally
b/c = because	4EAE = forever and ever
<3 = heart, or love	YATB = you are the best
@}->-- = rose	LYLAS = love ya like a sister
0:-) = angel	ppl = people
QT = cutie	Q4U = question for you
KC = keep cool	

Live. . .Luv. . .n LOL!!!

God is w/ u 24/7!

U r beautiful, grl!

Grls come n all shapes n sizes.
U r perfect n God's eyes!

A grl like u is a gr8 friend!

Shine ur light 2day!
The world needs more grls like u!

Wen I count my blessings,
I count u twice!

U make the world a betr place just by being u!

Jesus is ur BFF!

B4 u were born the world was missing 1 cool grl.

The LORD says,
"I will guide you along
the best pathway for your life.
I will advise you and watch
over you."

PSALM 32:8 NLT

B all that u can b 2day!

uRD1!

$$(((H)))$$

JTLYK I think u r a smart, cool grl.

Thx 4 being u.

Sending u a BG 2day.

G/F, u r so much fun!

4 God so loved the world that He gav His 1 n only Son 4 u!

U r 2 special!

*So encourage each other
and build each other up,
just as you are already doing.*

1 Thessalonians 5:11 NLT

A DF is 1 u can be urself with all the time.

I <333 U.

POAHF 2day,
n have a good 1.

*The world is betr
b/c u r n it!*

Grls like u r few n far between!

This <3 is 4 u.

u got grl power!

U can b anything u want to be!

I believe n u!

*Your love for one another
will prove to the world that you
are my disciples.*

JOHN 13:35 NLT

4get the bad, n hold
on2 the good in ur life!

Nevr 4get how much
God Luvs u!

u can if u think u can!

*Make a good day gr8
by just being u!*

Trust God 2 lead the way;
then follow.

Nevr giv up on ur dreams!

Believe in urself!
u will do gr8 things!

Attitude is supr important!
A good attitude can change ur day!

*U will nevr regret
doing the rite thing!*

God cares for you, so turn all your worries over to him.

1 PETER 5:7 CEV

Hav a gr8 day,
n remember u r 1 cool grl!

Ur so sweet!

2 the whole world ur somebody,
but 2 somebody ur the whole world!

2day is ur day, grl!

FRIENDS FOREVER ❀ FRIENDS FOREVER ❀ FRIENDS FOREVER ❀ FRIENDS FOREVER

@}->-- Sending u a rose!

*May God bless u, give u peace,
luv u, n cause u 2 shine 4 Him!*

U have many gifts n talents.
Use them 2day.

:-):-):-):-):-):-):-)

Enuf smiles 2 last 1 week!

If friends were flowers,
I wud pik u!

For God so loved the world that he gave his one and only Son, that whoever believes in him shall not perish but have eternal life.

JOHN 3:16 NIV

u r a 1 of a kind original, grl.

U r a true 0:-)!

Reach 4 the stars,
n ur dreams will come true!

Grl u r a treasure
n the <3s of many.

Ur beautiful inside n out.

Ur a winner, grl!

Wen u fall down,
get up n try again!
Don't let the world get u down!

u r a QT pie!

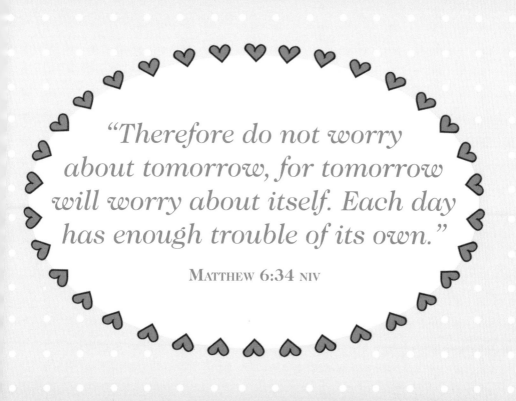

"Therefore do not worry about tomorrow, for tomorrow will worry about itself. Each day has enough trouble of its own."

MATTHEW 6:34 NIV

Remember who u r.
Remember who u represent.

Don't 4get 2 show luv
n all that u do 2day.

Roses r red; violets r blue.
This txt is 2 say God luvs u.

*Don't choose 2 sit out wen
u can choose 2 dance!*

Grls r special 2 the <3 of God.

2moro is a new day.
U get a fresh start!

KC grl.

Thx 4 being 1 gr8 grl.

A3 Jesus is on ur side!

In peace I will lie down and sleep,
for you alone, LORD,
make me dwell in safety.

PSALM 4:8 NIV

U deserve ATB n the world.

Sometimes a good HRT2HRT
is all 2 friends need.

u r a real sweet<3.

FYI ur 1NAM.

Giv some1 a hug 2day.
Evry1 needs luv!

B kind 2 ur family 2day.
They r ur 4ever friends.

2day give the world a gift
by smiling at every1 u c!

H&K 2 a supr star grl.

Ur a \&&&/.

*Make your light shine,
so that others will see the good
that you do and will praise
your Father in heaven.*

MATTHEW **5:16** CEV

U r nevr 2 young 2 luv big!

u r so talented at shopping, grl!

Jesus sez u r the lite of the world.
Shine 2day!

Dont 4get 2 stop n smell the roses 2day!

*Do something fun 2day. . .
just b/c u can!*

Always b urself.
ur the 1 God made u to b.

Ur the only u there could evr b!

If u have a <\3 take it 2 Jesus.
He is the 1 who can mend it!

Grl, u r amazing.

*Let us hold unswervingly
to the hope we profess,
for he who promised is faithful.*

HEBREWS 10:23 NIV

Sing n the shower.
Dance n the rain.
N always LOL!

Grl time is good 4 the soul!

If u r feeling blue,
try shopping 4 shoes.

Grls hav more fun!

*ROTFL is good 4
the <3 now n then.*

Don't 4get the 1s who luv u most.

Wen life givs u lemons,
make lemonade!

U r TTL cool.

Guard ur <3.

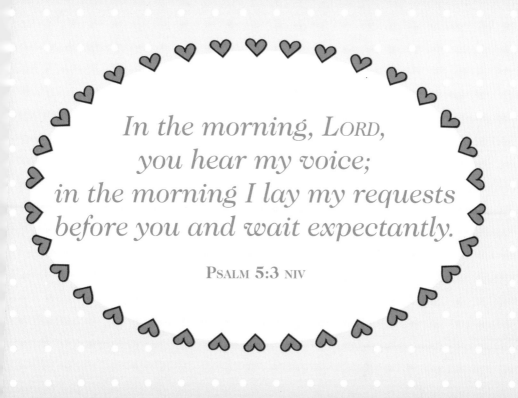

In the morning, LORD,
you hear my voice;
in the morning I lay my requests
before you and wait expectantly.

PSALM 5:3 NIV

*B/c u know Jesus,
u will liv 4EAE!*

God wants u 2 giv Him ur <3
so He can bless ur sox off!

FYI YATB!

God will c u thru!

It's EZ 2 c y I think ur 1 gr8 grl.
Just sayin. :-)

Ur 1 TTL awesome chick!

God luvs u more than
u can imagine!

Friends r like stars.
U can't always c them,
but u know they r always
there 4 u.

Wherever u go, whatever u do. . .
may God send an 0:-)
2 watch over u.

Charm is deceptive,
and beauty does not last;
but a woman who fears the LORD
will be greatly praised.

PROVERBS 31:30 NLT

B true 2 urself.

Ur true character shows
wen no1 is watching.

A friend looks out 4 u,
inspires u, laughs w/ u,
cries w/ u, n walks w/ u.
That's what a friend is. . .u.

*2day is a good day 2
do something 4 others!*

Grl, u make me :-).

2day is the 1st day of the rest of ur life!

G/Fs r 1 of the gr8est
blessings n life!

*Don't b afraid 2 sing
ur <3 out!*

Make new friends,
but keep the old.
1 is silver n the other gold.

*"For my thoughts are not
your thoughts, neither are your
ways my ways," declares the L*ORD*.
"As the heavens are higher than
the earth, so are my ways higher
than your ways and my thoughts
than your thoughts."*

ISAIAH 55:8–9 NIV

*Friends may come n go,
but family is 4ever.*

Honor ur mother n father.

The best way 2 b somebody
is to just b urself!

It's fun 2 LOL at urself now n then!

Don't settle 4 good.
W8 4 gr8!

Start ur day w/ prayer 2day.

Luv is n the litl things!

*Remember n the dark what
u learned n the lite!*

W/o pain there is no gain.
Hard work will pay off 4 u!

We love because
He first loved us.

1 JOHN 4:19 NIV

God luvs u just the way u r!

Problems r just
opportunities w/ thorns!

Make ur own sunshine 2day!

If u think u can, u probably can.
If u think u can't, u probably can't.

Instead of giving urself reasons y u can't. . .giv urself reasons y u can!

Do small things n a gr8 way!

No1 can go back n make a brand-new start, but any1 can start from now 2 make a brand-new ending!

Dream as if u will live 4ever,
live as if you'll die 2day.

JAMES DEAN

*If ur dream falls apart,
pick up the pieces!*

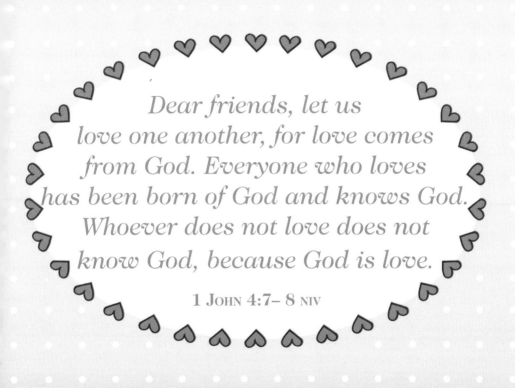

Dear friends, let us love one another, for love comes from God. Everyone who loves has been born of God and knows God. Whoever does not love does not know God, because God is love.

1 JOHN 4:7– 8 NIV

B not afraid 2 go slowly;
b afraid only of standing still.

Whatever u r, b a good 1.

ABRAHAM LINCOLN

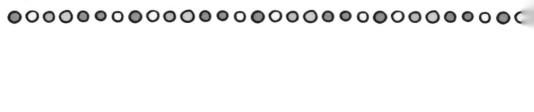

B the friend u want 2 have.

It is betr 2 give than 2 receive.

LYLAS, grl!

*Jesus is d way,
d truth, n d life!*

Always look 4 the best in ppl.

But the fruit of the Spirit is love, joy, peace, patience, kindness, goodness, faithfulness, gentleness, self-control; against such things there is no law.

GALATIANS 5:22–23 NASB

God's message 4 u:
Luv u! u r Mine!

Always think b4 u speak.

4give n 4get.
70 x 7.

*B the change u want
2 c in the world.*

Q4U. . . Did u get my txts?
I hope u r encouraged! <3